Dogs

of the National Trust

AMY FELDMAN

First published in the United Kingdom in 2019 by
National Trust Books
43 Great Ormond Street
London WC1N 3HZ
An imprint of Pavilion Books Company Ltd

ISBN: 9781911358695

A CIP catalogue record for this book is available from
the British Library.

25 24 23 22 21 20 19
10 9 8 7 6 5 4 3 2 1

Reproduction by Rival Colour Ltd, UK
Printed and bound by Toppan Leefung, China

This book can be ordered direct from the publisher
at the website: www.pavilionbooks.com, or try your
local bookshop.

MIX
Paper from
responsible sources
FSC® C104723
www.fsc.org

Right: *Mrs
Ferguson's Five
Puppies*, a portrait
by Chambré
Hardman (see
page 7).

Dogs

of the National Trust

AMY FELDMAN

INTRODUCTION

Dog and man have been devoted companions for millennia. In Northern Israel there is a grave dating to c.12,000BC in which an elderly man was buried alongside his puppy. To the Ancient Greeks they were geniuses and 'worthy of wonder' (Plato) and the Tarascans of pre-Colombian Mexico believed spirit dogs would look after the souls of those who died without a proper burial. Dogs have been beloved characters in books and films and have even become part of our political histories: most people know that, on winning the 2008 presidential election, Barack Obama used his speech to tell his daughters that they had 'earned the new puppy that's coming with us to the White House.'

And they are a part of our families and family lore too: in our household, no Christmas for the past decade-and-a-half has been complete without a re-telling of the day Lulu, a golden Cocker Spaniel, excavated the leftover turkey carcass from the bin (and spent the next week regurgitating it). I never met Buttons, but I know how she was gifted to my father's family – brought to them in a little box – and doted upon despite her penchant for biting imperiously at their heels on a regular basis.

Of course, many of the families who resided in National Trust places were no different, displaying portraits of their pets and writing down amusing anecdotes about them in letters and diaries. It was a treat to delve into these histories, to uncover tales of pups running riot through grand stately homes or terrorising guests, or to read books and poetry in which famous figures – Virginia Woolf, Vita Sackville-West and Thomas Hardy among them – wrote enthusiastically about dogs.

It was also a joy to meet some of the canine colleagues who live and work at National Trust places today. To see how some even help the Trust's conservation work, such as the sheepdogs that make sure the right places are grazed to allow wildlife to flourish. And then there are others whose goofy smiles and carefree antics make them essential companions and mood boosters for staff, volunteers and visitors alike. In fact, at The Argory in County Armagh, one tiny dog even volunteers as a Staff Morale Officer (see page 14).

While these dogs' temperaments, breeds and roles at National Trust places are many and varied, it was soon clear there was one thing they all had in common: just as the Famous Five would not be right without Timmy, Obama's White House without Bo the Portuguese Water Dog or our family's Christmas without the story of Lulu, these dogs too had become an integral, beloved chapter in the stories of their adopted National Trust workplaces and homes.

The Photographers' Muses

THE HARDMANS AND THEIR DOGS

59 Rodney Street, Liverpool

For Liverpudlians between the 1920s and 1960s, Edward Chambré Hardman (1898–1988) was the go-to portrait photographer. Yet if it wasn't for his father, he might not have taken up photography at all. 'I had an aptitude for science and mathematics but was not particularly interested in art,' Edward said of his boyhood self. His father, however, was a keen amateur who enjoyed snapping his family and pets, and he encouraged his son to experiment with a camera. Edward processed his first glass plates in the family's wine cellar and made contact prints in their apple loft.

Chambré Hardman's later business was a significant step up from this modest beginning. He had a studio on Liverpool's Bold Street before moving to Rodney Street in 1949, where he was surrounded by consultants and close to the birthplace of William Gladstone (number 62). These studios were where he took his portraits, of people and also of their pets: 'Miss Day', ready to pet a small dog standing on its hind legs; Mr and Mrs McDonald's sombre Spaniel; a basket of five Dachshund puppies (see page 1).

It was at Bold Street where, in 1926, Edward met 17-year-old Margaret. She was to be his apprentice, arriving straight out of school with a lifelong interest in photography and – according

Left: Hardman's portrait of Bicky Worcester, more commonly known as Bick.

to journalist Maev Kennedy – a 'glowing' reference from her headmistress. She later left for a job in Scotland, but the pair stayed in touch. By 1932 they were married, and Margaret had returned to Liverpool to help run the studio.

Margaret was integral to the business, looking after the finances, employees and clients. Her vibrant personality and glamorous wardrobe, complete with colourful jewellery and high-heeled wellies, left an impression upon staff and customers alike. She remained a passionate photographer, taking thousands of her own distinctive and dramatic images. Indeed, Edward once said that he 'could not have done it without her'.

The Hardmans were not only devoted to one another, but also to their pet dogs, who appear in many of their photographs. Bick, whom the Hardmans owned in the 1920s, was also a handy member of Bold Street staff, entertaining children as they waited and sometimes even appearing as a model alongside them. The dogs even posed in portraits of all the studio staff. Clearly they were very much a part of the Hardmans' loving world.

*The Work
of Art*

THE CARVED DOG BED

575 Wandsworth Road, London

Late Georgian townhouses like 575 Wandsworth Road are plentiful in London. Beyond this particular front door, however, you enter another world. Every room of the former home of Kenyan-born poet and civil servant Khadambi Asalache (1935–2006) is decorated with his hand-carved fretwork, inspired by buildings such as the *yali* that line the shores of the Bosphorus in Istanbul, and the Alhambra and the Great Mosque of Córboda in Andalusia. In each room, figures, patterns and animals dance over the walls and the edges of furniture and shelves.

Initially prompted by the need to disguise persistent damp in the basement dining room, Khadambi began to carve fretwork using pine salvaged from skips. He also carved his own furniture, including an intricate dog bed, which was intended for his girlfriend's Tibetan Spaniel, Ailsa. The dog bed, which was also a bedside table, was cut down from a larger piece. It has its own arched door and windows, one carved with a silhouette of swans. As the bed was slightly raised, Khadambi made Ailsa a stool from a wine crate and decorated it with a row of delicate figures holding hands. Ailsa, however, declined to use it.

Khadambi didn't just produce furniture for Ailsa. A closer look just above the skirting board on the stairs reveals a playful scene of antelopes, painted especially to give the dog something edifying to enjoy on her journeys up and down.

Right: The intricate wooden dog bed and bedside table, with the stool leading up to it, carved for Ailsa, the Tibetan Spaniel.

The Famous Messenger

'BUNGEY', THE FAVOURITE DOG OF SIR JOHN HARINGTON

Anglesey Abbey, Cambridgeshire

Queen Elizabeth I's godson, Sir John Harington (c.1560–1612), had a number of claims to fame. He invented the flush toilet (although it didn't become widely used until two centuries later), was a translator and writer, and was banished from court after circulating a lewd verse he'd translated among the court ladies. The story goes that his godmother agreed to allow him to return once he'd translated the 33,000-line epic poem, *Orlando Furioso*. Harington completed his much-lauded translation in 1591, and in the original his portrait appears on the opening page, alongside his beloved dog Bungey.

Bungey was no ordinary pooch. Writing to James I's son Prince Henry in 1608, Harington described how his pet delivered communications from his home in Kelston, near Bath, to court in London. Another time, Bungey carried two flaskets (long, shallow baskets) the 4 miles (6.4km) from Bath to his master's house. During the journey, the tie holding the flaskets together came apart and Bungey, lacking opposable thumbs, couldn't rectify this. So he hid one in some rushes, dragged the other to Kelston, and then returned to the hiding place to complete the delivery, all to the marvel of onlooking field workers.

Subsequently, Bungey became famous, but this brought unwanted attention; he was once stolen by rustlers, who sold him to the Spanish Ambassador. The distraught John eventually won him back by performing a trick with Bungey, thereby proving his ownership.

Left: 'Bungey', the favourite dog of Sir John Harington. This portrait, which can now be seen at Anglesey Abbey, dates from c.1800.

The Tiniest Volunteer

BISCUIT

The Argory,
County Armagh

The Argory's second owner, Captain Ralph Shelton (1832–1916), kept a rather unusual log of his guests: a book listing the weight of each one to the nearest ounce. This wasn't limited to humans. Inked into the pages are records for four dogs belonging to his great nephew, Mr Bond – Bill, Boxer, Jess and Pat – and even for Captain Shelton's own Jack Russell Terrier, Vic. Vic's grave can be seen in The Argory's grounds.

Although The Argory no longer continues this practice, one current volunteer could undoubtedly challenge for the title of lightest-ever visitor. Biscuit the Jug (a Jack Russell/Pug cross) was just 1lb (450g) when he first started here as a part-time Staff Morale Officer. Then just eight weeks old, he has since grown, but will always be one of the Trust's smallest volunteers.

Biscuit may be little, but he quickly became a big part of The Argory. So much so that his role was created especially for him after his owner, House Steward Matthew Morrison, started to bring him on visits and the team realised how happy the little Jug made everyone. Biscuit's morale-boosting talents aren't limited to The Argory; he went viral after a photograph of him proudly wearing his staff badge was shared over 150,000 times online (and counting).

Left: Biscuit is coping well with internet stardom and loves posing for photographs, meeting fans and generally being the centre of attention.

The Lost Statue

THE DOG OF ALCIBIADES

Basildon Park, Berkshire; Blickling Hall, Norfolk; Petworth, West Sussex

In the mid-18th century, when British antiquarian Henry Constantine Jennings was living in Rome, he happened across the workshop of sculptor and art dealer Bartolomeo Cavaceppi. There, in a pile of rubble, Jennings noticed a 1m (41in) marble sculpture of a seated dog with a docked tail. Jennings bought the piece for about £80 and brought it with him to Britain. The statue, which dates from AD2, is one of very few Roman sculptures of animals to have survived and is now in the British Museum.

The dog is a now-extinct breed, a Molossian guard dog, which heralded from ancient southern Europe. The sculpture itself is probably a copy of a now-lost Hellenistic bronze original. Jennings christened it 'The Dog of Alcibiades' because of its broken tail – Alcibiades was an Athenian statesman who allegedly cut off his dog's tail so that Athenians would make fun of the animal instead of him. The statue is also sometimes known as 'The Jennings Dog', named after the man who discovered it.

Various replicas of the statue have since been made and can be spotted at National Trust properties including Basildon Park in Berkshire, Petworth Park in West Sussex and Blickling Hall in Norfolk. The latter was commissioned by Lady Constance in 1877 and she appears to have had a particular fondness for the piece; a smaller version – perhaps a souvenir from her travels – can also be found inside the house.

Left: The dog of Alcibiades statue at Blickling Hall, Norfolk.

The Treasured Terriers

RUDYARD KIPLING AND HIS MANY DOGS

Bateman's,
East Sussex

Vixen the Fox Terrier was seemingly loyal to one man in particular. In the 1880s, Rudyard Kipling (1865–1936) was working in India. During one trip home, he and Vixen became companions, but he had to return to India, and so his mother and sister took on responsibility for the 'fat, white waddler'. Vixen's was more than a cupboard love, however; as soon as he returned, Vixen transferred her allegiance straight back to the writer.

Kipling was a lifelong dog-lover, something that is clear to visitors to Bateman's both past and present: there's the Scottie-adorned ashtray and wooden matchbox on his desk (he kept many Scotties there); the commemorative gravestones; the chew-marks still visible on legs of stools and tables.

He passed on his affection for the animals to his children, Jack and Elsie. When they were small, Kipling would rearrange the furniture in the parlour so they could play on the floor with their pets. In 1910 he acquired two Terriers, Jack and Betty, and noted how Elsie, then 14, was 'awfully good with the dogs and … dries their little feet after they have been running in the wet grass'. She continued to love dogs in adulthood (see page 123).

After his children left home, Kipling owned a number of Aberdeen Terriers; a photograph of one can still be seen in the study. These included James who was, according to politician Thelma Cazalet-Keir, a 'special favourite' who 'always lay under the table with his head on his master's feet'. In 1932, James was joined by Malachi. Kipling told

Right: Rudyard Kipling with James the Terrier in 1934.

Buy a pup and your money will buy
Love unflinching that cannot lie ...

RUDYARD KIPLING, 'THE POWER OF THE DOG'

Left: Rudyard Kipling at Bateman's with two small black dogs, c.1934. Carrie Kipling can be seen in the background.

his sister that taking the two for walks was 'like trying to co-ordinate a bath-chair and a baby-Austin'. Malachi would usually be found with a toy in his mouth, or waiting with a mournful expression until Kipling would consent to play fetch.

Dogs also inspired Kipling's writing – so much so that in the 1930s he published three anthologies of his canine works. The public lapped them up; the first collection, *Thy Servant a Dog*, sold 100,000 copies in six months.

Critics are divided on their quality, however. 'Few major writers have written so bad a book: almost none in their maturity,' asserted author Martin Fido. A former editor of the *Kipling Journal* was more measured, saying the stories were 'unusual but amusing', but added 'no extra glory' to Kipling's otherwise impressive catalogue. A more contemporary review in *The Times* takes a different perspective: 'The superior and the humourless may find Mr Kipling's stories of dogs light or even trivial entertainment, but those who know how to enter into their spirit will be very content with them … they are deft and charming, bubbling with fun, touched with pathos, full of acute observation'. Just the way a book about dogs should be.

'NO ONE APPRECIATES
THE VERY SPECIAL GENIUS
OF YOUR CONVERSATION
AS THE DOG DOES.'

CHRISTOPHER MORLEY

The Legend

GELERT THE BRAVE

Beddgelert, Gwynedd

Just outside of the Snowdonian village of Beddgelert, in the shade of a tree, is the spot after which the village is named: what is thought to be the grave of Gelert the dog. Here, so says the legend, lies the body of this fearless hound, who once belonged to a brave and well-liked medieval prince, Llywelyn the Great. At the time of this story, Prince Llywelyn was heartbroken, the mother of his child having died in childbirth. His young baby was his only consolation.

Gelert was faithful to the Prince, accompanying him everywhere. But one day, Llywelyn went out without the dog, leaving him instead to protect his home and baby. On Llywelyn's return he was greeted by a terrible sight: his son's cot was empty and overturned, the furs that had covered it shredded and scattered, and Gelert was smeared with blood. Believing the worst, Llewelyn plunged his sword into his dog.

As Gelert lay dying, Llywelyn heard a cry: it was his son. The boy had been hidden by the upturned cradle. As Llywelyn picked up the baby he noticed the dead body of a huge wolf: Gelert had saved the child but it was too late; Gelert was dead. Llywelyn buried him with great ceremony in the spot now marked by a stone slab and sculpture. It is said that, overcome with remorse, the prince never smiled again.

Right: A bronze statue commemorates Gelert near the site of his grave at Beddgelert, Snowdonia.

The Friendly Thief

ROGER

Birling Gap,
East Sussex

Volunteer briefings at Birling Gap often include a rather unusual instruction: secure your lunch bags. Those who fail to heed the warning may find that their food has disappeared – into the mouth of a Cocker Spaniel named Roger.

Roger was rescued in 2015 and has been working part-time with the Birling Gap Rangers ever since, usually twice a week. He quickly became fond of going on trips around the estate in the Rangers' truck, but is less of a fan of being cooped up in the office. This 'normally manifests itself in stealing from desks, handbags or generally anything that will get him a bit of attention', admits his owner, Ranger Ashley Dalleywater. And it's not just volunteers who need to watch their lunches. 'His daily routine includes bursting into the office and racing around all the desks to steal any unattended food before I can get to it!' Ashley reveals.

From the bright white chalk cliff face of the Seven Sisters to the plentiful rock pools on the shoreline, it's easy to see why Roger prefers exploring Birling Gap to being in the office. However, there is one downside to getting out and about: Roger's droopy ears are frequently covered in agrimony seeds. 'I often have to spend hours plucking these Velcro-like seeds from them when we get home!' says Ashley. We suspect Roger thinks this is a price worth paying for a day bounding around in the fresh sea air.

Left: Roger loves riding about in vehicles, especially around Birling Gap.

The Constant Companion

NERO AND THE CARLYLES

Carlyle's House, London

Right: *A Chelsea Interior* by Robert Tait (1857–8). Nero can be seen to the right, sitting on the sofa. In early versions, Jane said that Nero was 'the only member of the family to be pleased with his likeness'. Later on, however, the opposite was true, and Jane believed Nero appeared to be far too big.

Before Jane Welsh Carlyle (1801–66) married in 1826, her letters paid homage to another big part of her life: Shandy the Blenheim Cocker Spaniel, who featured not only in her stories, but sometimes in pictorial form too, in the waxy seal that closed her letters.

Jane loved Shandy so much that when she was gifted a new dog in December 1849 – a 'perfectly beautiful and queer' black-and-white mongrel she called Nero – she told her old nurse that 'no dog can ever replace dear little Shandy in my affections'.

However, it didn't take long for Nero to carve out a place in her heart. The following year Jane told a friend that he was 'the chief comforter of my life'. The cake-loving creature was smuggled on board trains and sat with her in a donkey chair as they journeyed round Hampstead Heath. She fed him sugar lumps, strawberries and tumblers of brandy, and spoke of him in her letters (he was sometimes also their 'author'). She once even wrote him a satirical love letter while she was away.

Jane's friends recognised Nero's importance to her. When he was stolen in 1851, Jane considered not paying the ransom so as not to encourage the thieves. Her friend intervened, urging her not to give up: 'He was the only thing that did not torment you.' In 1855, when Jane was going through a miserable time, she told a friend that she felt like 'retiring to bed, and abjuring my fellow creatures – all but Nero,' until she felt better.

At first, Jane's husband, the writer Thomas Carlyle (1795–1881), wasn't quite so taken with Nero; he frequently referred to him as a 'wretch'. He did harbour some affection for the little dog, however, amusedly describing his chasing imaginary birds in a letter; in another, their mutual joy on being reunited after the couple returned from a trip. Nero (or at least, Jane masquerading as Nero) would send him letters while he was away, and his wife noticed how the dog would cheer Thomas up by dancing round him on his hind legs.

A shared swim in the bitter North Sea cemented the bond between the pair, but unfortunately just a few months later Nero met his untimely end: when walking to the shops with the couple's maid, he was run over by a butcher's cart, his neck and lungs crushed. He survived the accident, but, after struggling through the winter, he had to be put down. Jane wrote to the vet to thank him for helping Nero, describing the feelings of the household. 'The grief his death has caused me has been wonderful even to myself,' she wrote, adding that Thomas's heart was '(as he phrased it) "unexpectedly and distractedly torn to pieces with it"'. 'I grieve for him as if he had been my little human child,' she added. For Nero was always more than a pet to Jane. As she said to Thomas in 1852, 'He is part and parcel of myself; when I say I am well, it means also Nero is well! *Nero c'est moi! Moi c'est Nero!*'

Right: Jane with her beloved Nero.

The Schmoozer

MAX

Charlecote Park,
Warwickshire

On Valentine's Day of 2018, a new social-media star was born. In a video celebrating one of the most unbreakable of bonds between 'master' and dog, Max, a gentle Collie cross with floppy ears and soulful eyes, melted hearts across the land as footage appeared of him bringing his owner, Ranger Joy Margerum, a beautiful bunch of flowers.

Despite his fame, Max has not developed diva tendencies: 'He's the same old Max,' says Joy, 'always looking for a fuss and a treat from staff, volunteers, visitors – whoever happens to be around!' A former rescue dog, he has assisted Joy in her role for a number of years, starting out at Attingham Park in Shropshire before moving to Charlecote in 2016. His (unofficial) duties there include hoovering up crumbs in the break room, allowing Rangers to use his long fur to warm their fingers in winter, modelling for National Trust photo shoots, and helping to unwrap presents by 'gently working a corner of paper up and then tearing it off'. He also loves chatting to fellow dog owners when they visit; 'He makes the perfect icebreaker,' says Joy.

When Max is off duty, he might be spotted chasing and chewing sticks, snoozing in the sun or 'lying legs akimbo, getting his belly rubbed'.

Left: Doe-eyed Max has got used to posing for the camera.

RUFUS AND CHURCHILL

Chartwell, Kent

Sir Winston Churchill's 79th birthday cake was an elaborate affair. Circling the base were the spines of each of his published works. On the top was a sugarcraft Poodle: Churchill's beloved dog, Rufus II, trying 'to clamber up the candle to reach a tiny cat at the top'.

This was, literally and figuratively, the icing on the cake of Churchill's lifelong love of animals. His menagerie at Chartwell included Middle White pigs, bantams that pecked at fallen crumbs on the dining-room floor, goats who ate their way through the flower borders, and black swans. But it was dogs and cats who reigned. Their presence is still felt at Chartwell today: in honour of Sir Winston's beloved ginger cat, Jock, his family asked that there always be a marmalade cat with four white paws and a white bib in residence, a request the Trust has honoured.

As his name suggests, Rufus II had a predecessor. Rufus was also a brown Poodle and rode everywhere with Churchill during the Second World War. He and Churchill's cats would roam 10 Downing Street, and Rufus once tried (unsuccessfully) to attend a wartime Cabinet Room meeting. His death in 1947 devastated Churchill, and he consoled himself by obtaining a second brown Poodle a few months later, Rufus II ('but the II is silent').

Left: Churchill and Rufus II at Chartwell in 1950.

But Churchill soon feared the worst for his new dog, who developed a 'distressing complaint' in January 1948. He wrote concernedly of his dog's health to Bella Lobban, the kennel owner who looked after Rufus II when Churchill was away, and also requested that she not look out for a new dog for him should the worst happen. 'After the sad loss of the first one, I feel that I would rather not have another dog just now,' he wrote. Fortunately his fears were not realised and Rufus II made a full recovery. He lived to be 15, and was buried next to his predecessor in Chartwell's grounds.

Rufus II was thoroughly spoilt by Churchill (and by Bella Lobban, who sent him gifts of leads, coats and collars on Churchill's birthdays); it's said he ate with the family in the dining room. Churchill shielded him from any distress, too. One evening the family were watching *Oliver Twist* and Sir Winston shielded Rufus II's eyes during the scene in which Bill Sykes drowns his Bull Terrier, Bullseye: 'Don't look now. I'll tell you about it afterwards,' Sir Winston reassured his Poodle.

In one of Churchill's most famous quotes, he expounds the virtues of pigs: 'Dogs look up to us. Cats look down on us. Pigs treat us as equals.' In reality, it seems Churchill doted on his dogs just as much as they would have doted upon him.

Right: Churchill's 79th birthday cake, featuring a sugarcraft Rufus II, being prepared in November 1953.

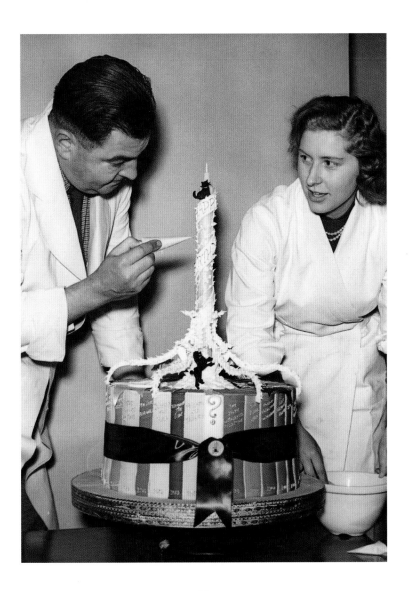

The Pug and the Patterjack

FERRIS AND MARPLE

Chastleton House and Garden, Oxfordshire

Chastleton – a Jacobean manor nestled in the Cotswold countryside – has a reputation for being a house of cats. The last owner before the Trust took over had no fewer than 20 (as well as a parrot), and the tradition of feline occupants continues today with Offa, Odo and Ottaline. Less well known is that today's cats have an unexpected ally and protector: Ferris the Patterjack (a Patterdale Terrier/Jack Russell cross).

Ferris, who trained for this role over five years at Coughton Court in Warwickshire (also National Trust), sweeps Chastleton's grounds every night. He keeps a particular eye out for the neighbourhood cats that try to sneak in and steal food from the resident pusses, but he also keeps tabs on any passing humans, watching them closely from the Brewhouse windowsill.

Ferris's canine colleague, Marple, works in custodial, helping to keep Chastleton clean and tidy. In other words, as her owner and Chastleton's Operations Manager Rebecca Farr puts it, she is 'a walking bin'. 'She is happy to help any passing visitor inspect their sandwiches and cakes and will cheerfully tidy up under the picnic tables,' says Rebecca of her jet-black Pug.

Right: Ferris (left) and Marple (right) guard the entrance to Chastleton.

Despite Chastleton being famous for its cats, Ferris and Marple are not the first dogs to have lived here. The Richardson family, who were residents from 1896–1933, were huge dog-lovers, especially the daughters. The pets appeared at events and in many family photographs – Winkyn, a black Spaniel, and Pip the Terrier were particularly popular with the camera – and three dog graves, commemorating Babette, Julie and Nankie, can still be seen on the terrace. So much a part of the family were they that when one sister, Veronica, got married in 1933, she had her favourite Whippet brought to Chastleton Church so that it could be the first to greet her as a married woman. The Whippet also features in the bridal photograph (shown here), sitting centre stage in front of the bride. We think the sisters would be pleased to know Ferris and Marple are continuing Chastleton's canine legacy.

Right: Veronica's bridal party in 1933 included her beloved Whippet.

10.

'THE GREAT PLEASURE
OF A DOG IS THAT YOU MAY
MAKE A FOOL OF YOURSELF
WITH HIM AND NOT ONLY
WILL HE NOT SCOLD YOU, BUT
HE WILL MAKE A FOOL
OF HIMSELF TOO.'

SAMUEL BUTLER

The Champions

KATHERINE PELHAM-CLINTON AND THE DOGS OF CLUMBER

Clumber Park, Nottinghamshire

In 1892, Tsar Nicholas II (then a Grand Duke) brought 16 Borzois to Britain to enter them into Crufts. They weren't the best Borzois of the bunch, but this didn't put off Kathleen Pelham-Clinton (1872–1955). The young Duchess of Newcastle paid a reported £200 for the best one – the equivalent of about £20,000 today. It was a worthwhile investment; she went on to become a renowned Borzoi breeder, producing eight champions.

Kathleen was also a revered dog-show judge, President of the Wire Fox Terrier Association, Chairman of the Ladies Branch of the Kennel Club (1899–1901) and produced 12 Wire Fox Terrier champions. By the 1890s she kept over 90 dogs in specially built dog kennels at Clumber Park, including the breed that took their name from her Nottinghamshire estate: Clumber Spaniels.

The Clumber Spaniel pre-dated Kathleen, though how it made its way to Britain is a mystery. One story is that the Duc de Noailles gave his dogs to the Duke of Newcastle to save them during the French Revolution. The less romantic explanation is that Clumber was always home to Spaniels, but other breeds were imported from Europe to adapt them for work in nearby Sherwood Forest.

Under Clumber's gamekeeper William Mansell, the square-headed dog – the largest of all Spaniels – became one of the most fashionable breeds of the day, kept by royalty and aristocracy. However, Clumbers roam no more on the estate: the last, Basil, left around the turn of the millennium.

Left: Kathleen Pelham-Clinton with one of her champion Borzoi.

The Prized Pugg

THE BOOTHS AND THEIR MASTIFFS

Dunham Massey, Cheshire

Right: *Old Vertue*, the favourite Dutch Mastiff of George Booth and his daughter Mary, painted by Jan Wyck, oil on canvas, (1700). As well as the prominent likeness in the foreground, Old Vertue can also be seen in the background, chasing sheep. This shows Dunham Massey before George had it rebuilt in the 1700s.

It is said that George Booth, the 2nd Earl of Warrington (1675–1758) loved his dogs more than his wife. While the walls of Dunham Massey are filled with portraits of his pets, there is not a single image of his wife, Mary Oldbury.

Admittedly the couple's 38-year marriage was an unhappy one: Mary left her friends, family and a life of comfort to live in what was then a tumbledown manor (George later restored it). The absence of a portrait of Mary, therefore, is not that surprising, but the presence of dog portraits is more unusual – in George's day, the nobility often had their racehorses painted, but rarely their dogs. And while pet cemeteries are no longer uncommon in grand houses, Dunham Massey's is thought to be one of the earliest; the oldest surviving grave, for 'Pugg, alias Old Vertue', dates from 1702.

A love of dogs seems to have run in the Booth family. In 1682, George's cousin Katherine (1672–1765), added a codicil to her will: 'I cannot satisfie myself without taking care of my sensible loving Dutch Masive Poppet if I die before her' and left from her estate 'twelve pence a week to maintain her in meat'. Further instructions included providing Poppet with bread and a coffee cup of milk at breakfast, allowing her to sleep on the bed should she so wish, and stating that she should be 'first thing carried out to some place in a morning to doe her occasions'.

The Conservation Collies

LOTTIE, LEXI AND CHIP

Formby, Liverpool

If you're off for a day relaxing on the beach at Formby, don't be surprised if you see a gaggle of Collies patrolling the area alongside the human Rangers. These are Lottie, Lexi and Chip, known collectively as the 'Conservation Collies'. Together the three enjoy meeting visitors and teaching their dogs all about how to behave appropriately on an important conservation site. Another very important duty is helping to keep the Formby Rangers smiling through good days and tougher ones.

Of the three, Lottie, a rescue dog, is the longest-standing Formby employee, having started working there full-time in 2014. She loves a game of Frisbee on Formby's wide stretch of sand, cooling off in the sea, playing 'tag' with Chip and watching the rabbits scamper about in the Rangers' yard. She's also got an independent streak: 'Lottie has a tendency to take herself off on walks with other people,' says her owner Kate Martin. 'It's not unusual for me to get a radio call from a colleague or volunteer who Lottie has tagged along with.' Her appetite is also renowned among Formby staff. If she's not running around outside, or napping curled up against her best friend Lexi, she can usually be found in the Rangers' mess room, trying to steal a bite to eat.

With Lottie's older age and wisdom comes great responsibility: keeping the youngest of the pack, energetic Chip, in check. Chip arrived at Formby

Left: Chip, one of the 'Conservation Collies' patrolling the beach at Formby.

in 2016, then a 9-month-old rescue puppy. Bouncy
and boisterous, he sometimes annoys his canine
colleagues, but Lottie will soon sort him out with
a gentle whack. This 'works for about five minutes',
admits Chip's human, Rob.

The third member of this motley crew is Lexi,
who started coming to work part-time as a member
of the Visitor Experience team in 2015 and became
a full-time 'Conservation Collie' two years later.
She is the shyest of the trio (if you spot a dog
hiding behind a Ranger then it's probably Lexi), but
her best friend, Lottie, has helped her come out of
her shell. Lexi loves performing tricks, swimming in
the sea before 'drying off' in the sand, and stealing
dog toys from Lottie and Chip in the yard (Lottie
enjoys this game – Chip less so). A born Ranger,
she also loves going for a ride in the Land Rover.
'[She] is usually the first in the team to jump in
them of a morning. She likes to stick her head out
of the window to make sure she doesn't miss any
good smells along the coast,' says Isabelle Spall,
Lexi's owner. Her love of riding in cars doesn't stop
here, however: 'she will readily jump in any of the
Rangers' cars if it looks like they're going for a
drive!' Isabelle reveals.

The Order of the Faithful Dogs

AGATHA CHRISTIE'S BELOVED DOGS

Greenway, Devon

One of the first known photographs of Agatha Christie (1890–1976) is of her aged five, clutching a scruffy mutt known as George Washington. She went on to own many a Terrier, particularly Airedales and Manchesters. The last of these, Bingo, 'bit everybody but was still loved', reminisces her grandson, Mathew Prichard in his series of videos, 'The Essence of Agatha Christie' (2014). Many of her treasured OFDs (Order of the Faithful Dogs) now rest in a dedicated cemetery in the fernery at Greenway – her peaceful Devonshire holiday home and her 'dream house', where she escaped from work and the world.

The animals are present in her writing, too. In the short story 'Next to a Dog', a poor widow fights to keep her half-blind Terrier, Terry, who was a gift from her late husband. In *The Moving Finger*, Christie writes that 'Dogs are wise. They crawl away into a quiet corner and lick their wounds and do not rejoin the world until they are whole once more.' But perhaps her most famous canine character appears in the Hercule Poirot mystery, *Dumb Witness*.

In this, the dumb witness of the title is a Wire Fox Terrier named Bob. Bob belongs to a murdered housewife and for a time is suspected of unwittingly causing his mistress's death by leaving

Left: Agatha Christie in the 1920s. Christie kept many Terriers and one of them, her Wire Fox Terrier, Peter, even appeared on the cover of her book *Dumb Witness*.

53

> 'Whenever you think you haven't got a friend in the world and nothing is going right, one look at your dog and you feel that the world is a slightly better place.'

MATHEW PRICHARD, CHRISTIE'S GRANDSON

his ball at the top of the stairs. The character is based upon Christie's affectionate real-life Terrier, Peter, who appeared on the cover and, in some editions, in illustrations throughout. The book is also famously dedicated, 'To dear Peter, most faithful of friends and dearest of companions, a dog in a thousand.'

It is perhaps unsurprising then that, according to Mathew, it was Peter who was 'Possibly the [dog] she loved best … [he was] affectionate and cemented her relationship with the species.' Peter appears to have reciprocated her affections. In December 1926, Christie became the subject of her own, real-life mystery when she disappeared for 11 days; a highly publicised search ensued before she was discovered in a hotel in Harrogate. The events took place during a particularly traumatic time in her life, after her first husband left her and her mother died, and she was clearly shaken. On her return home, Mathew describes how it was Peter 'who met her as a long-lost friend as if she'd never been away; he wagged his tail, [and] she felt for one moment normal again.'

Left: The love of dogs ran in the family; painted in 1893, this Dandie Dinmont, named Scotty, belonged to 'Monty' Miller, Christie's elder brother.

The Tale of a Slow-burning Love

BEATRIX POTTER AND KEP

Hill Top, Cumbria

'I do not on the average care for dogs – especially other people's,' declared a young Beatrix Potter (1866–1943). Slowly though, with every summer her family spent in the Lake District, the animals worked their way into her affection.

But it wasn't until 1907, when Beatrix took over her own Lake District farm, that her love affair with the animals truly began. This is the year Kep arrived, along with six dairy cows. While most of Beatrix's Collies worked on the farm, one was always more of a pet, as was the case with Kep. A year later, she made him the hero of *The Tale of Jemima Puddle-Duck*, in which he rescues the naïve bird from the jaws of a hungry fox.

Kep, who died in 1917, was succeeded by Fleet the Bobtail. Later came Nip, whose offspring included Fly. Fly was initially frightened of sheep and had to be trained on hens ('this is not as naughty as it looks, she never bites! … She sometimes put them in the hen hut,' insisted Beatrix).

From the smiling photos of Beatrix with her dogs, from the affectionate portraits of them in her letters and diaries, stories and sketches, it's clear the Collies well and truly won her over.

Right: Beatrix Potter with Kep at Hill Top in 1907 or 1908.

The Helpful Guide

FRANK AND THE DOG HOUSE

Ightham Mote, Kent

Of all the Grade I listed buildings in England and Wales, Ightham Mote is surely home to one of the most unusual: an outdoor dog kennel. It was created for Sir Thomas Colyer-Fergusson (1865–1951), who moved to Ightham Mote in 1889 and set about modernising the building, adding central heating and a bathroom. But it is the 2m (6½ft) long stone-built dog house in the courtyard that is his most intriguing addition. Its vast dimensions are down to the size of its first occupant, Dido the St Bernard. The next occupants were somewhat less in need of the space, though – two Pekingese dogs named Mr Ping and Mr Pong.

Although dogs no longer visit the Mote's courtyard, some do still live and work here. Frank, a Golden Labrador, first started out as a guide dog for a volunteer tour guide. He quickly made himself comfortable; once when the tour guide was in a meeting, Frank was taken for a walk by some fellow volunteers and leapt into the moat.

Frank has since retired as a guide dog, but he loved Ightham Mote so much – a feeling reciprocated by the staff – that he went on to live with the Retail Manager. He is now an important member of the shop team and can be found greeting and entertaining visitors most days.

Right: Ightham Mote's Victorian dog kennel.

The Board Game Hero

TOBY

Killerton, Devon

One New Year, when Toby's human Fi Hailstone, a Nature Officer at Killerton, was playing National Trust Monopoly, she came in for quite a surprise. Out of the blue, a friend drew a Community Chest card featuring her pet, Toby the Ranger dog. In this edition of the famous game the recipient of this card receives £100 in monopoly money after 'Toby is photographed driving a National Trust Land Rover and becomes a social-media sensation.'

A working Cocker Spaniel, Toby hasn't let his new-found stardom get in the way of his responsibilities at Killerton. He's been here since September 2015, when he was just a pup, and spends his days with Fi and the Ranger team as they work out in the woods, orchards and farmland. His favourite job, though, is butterfly surveying because, as Fi puts it, 'He gets a long walk in the sunshine and helps by "putting the butterflies up"'; when Toby runs through the grass, the butterflies are disturbed and fly up into the air, making them easier to count. In his free time he loves to get out and about on Exmoor or to curl up in front of a log burner.

While Toby is a valued member of the Killerton team, he does also have a mischievous streak, particularly when it comes to food, and has been known to steal the boss's sandwiches.

Left: Toby during Killerton's Apple Week.

'KNOW YOURSELF. DON'T
ACCEPT YOUR DOG'S
ADMIRATION AS CONCLUSIVE
EVIDENCE THAT YOU ARE
WONDERFUL.'

ANN LANDERS

The Turnspits and the Kokoni

THE DOG WHEEL

Lacock, Wiltshire

Pay a visit to the 14th-century George Inn pub at Lacock and you might spot an unusual wooden wheel set into the wall: this was once the workplace of hardworking Turnspit dogs.

Roasting meat on a spit over an open fire was a typical medieval cooking method, but without fan ovens to ensure even heating, the meat had to be constantly turned by hand. Originally this task was given to low-ranking servants, but it later became the responsibility of specially bred Turnspits with their short legs and long, muscular bodies.

Turnspits' diminutive stature and the disproportionate weight and strength of their bodies made them the perfect shape to run, hamster-like, inside these dog wheels. The wheels were attached to the spit by a chain, and the dog's movement ensured the spit, and thus the meat, rotated evenly. In larger kitchens, a couple of Turnspits might share the arduous task. They were also sometimes relieved of their duties on Sundays – but allegedly only so they could be foot-warmers in church. As can be seen in the George Inn, the wheels were set high up on the wall to keep the dogs away from the fire and prevent them from overheating, but this probably had more to do with productivity rather than concern for the dogs' welfare.

Tales abound about these unfortunate hounds: how they knew exactly when their shift was due to finish and would leap out regardless of whether their companion was there to relieve them; dogs

Right: The medieval dog wheel at Lacock's George Inn.

refusing to work; and even dogs who would kill their canine colleague if forced to work instead of them (though most of this is probably folklore).

Both technology and animal cruelty legislation have improved since then; Turnspits had disappeared from kitchens by around 1900, and today Lacock's dog wheel is for show only. This is good news for Lacock's current canine residents: a large black Retriever cross called Oscar, and Lily, a Kokoni who came to Lacock in September 2017. Although Lily is always active, we think she'd prefer to stick to racing around the grounds (or running rings around Oscar – who does a good job of pretending she isn't there) over the dog wheel.

Catch Lily in a calmer moment (most likely on Lacock Abbey's East Terrace on her lunchtime walk) and she'll be more than happy to stop for a chat, or to shake your hand in exchange for a treat. She's very particular about where you stroke her though. Stray too far from her favourite spot (where her front legs join her body) and she'll carefully push your hand back to where she wants it and hold it in place. If only the Turnspits of Lacock could see how dogs are treated here now …

Left: Lily the Kokoni explores a snowy Lacock.

The Snowdonia Shepherdess

ROY AND TELERI

Llyndy Isaf Farm, Snowdonia

When Roy took on the role of sheepdog at Llyndy Isaf farm, he didn't expect this to lead him to the BBC Breakfast sofa. Yet after he appeared alongside his young boss, Teleri Fielden, in *Snowdonia Shepherdess* – a 2018 documentary about her scholarship at the 600-acre (243-hectare) North Wales National Trust farm – both suddenly found themselves in the limelight.

That hasn't distracted Roy from his daily duties, which include rounding up sheep on the rocky hillside, helping Teleri when she works in the pens and keeping her company. Both Teleri and Roy have learnt on the job (with help from those working at nearby National Trust farm, Hafod y Llan), but it's not all been plain sailing: 'Within farming you have to expect the unexpected, so you have to have a sense of humour about things going wrong,' says Teleri.

She recalls one such event from early in their career. The pair were working with the Hafod y Llan team on a big mountain gather, but Roy had only ever moved sheep in a field before. 'Right at the end, when we had nearly all the sheep (hundreds of them) gathered near the bottom, he decided that he needed to push them back up the mountain for me,' Teleri recalls. 'The sheep weren't very impressed with this new young dog and ignored him. I eventually found him sulking by the side!'

Right: Teleri and Roy look out over the Snowdonia hills.

68

The Terrible Terrier

THE HARDYS AND WESSEX

Max Gate, Dorset

Wessex was 'the most despotic dog guests had ever suffered under', declared Lady Cynthia Asquith of Thomas and Florence Hardy's scruffy Fox Terrier. The white-haired, brown-eared pooch – a descendant of Edward VII's favourite dog, Caesar – was infamous in his day. He attacked guests' legs, destroyed their trousers, and waltzed across the table at dinner to try to steal food from their forks. He terrorised the servants and one guest, Sir John Collings Squire, observed how Wessex held Thomas Hardy hostage in the dining room until he turned on the wireless.

Yet Thomas wasn't that taken with Wessex when Florence acquired him in 1913. According to their cook, Mrs Stanley, he told his wife, 'Two things that you have brought into this house that I dislike are the dog Wessex and Mrs Stanley's child.' But it wasn't long before Thomas was taking Wessex on trips, feeding him goose and plum pudding at Christmas and, according to Florence, kissing him before bed each night.

So when Wessex passed away in December 1926, aged 13, both Florence and Thomas were distraught; Thomas even wrote two poems dedicated to their tempestuous Terrier. Wessex was buried in Max Gate's garden and in his diary, Thomas mourned: 'Wx sleeps outside the house for the first time for 13 years.' His gravestone, which can still be seen at Max Gate, was designed by Thomas and provides a fitting epitaph: 'The Famous Dog Wessex; Faithful, Unflinching.'

Left: Thomas, Florence and Wessex at Max Gate.

> 'A dog somehow represents ... the private side of life – the play side.'

VIRGINIA WOOLF

A Flush of Dogs

THE WOOLFS AND THEIR DOGS

Monk's House,
East Sussex

Right: Vita
Sackville-West
and Virginia Woolf
with Pinka and
another Spaniel.

One of the most unexpected books in Virginia Woolf's *oeuvre* was, in its time, one of her most popular. *Flush*, a fictionalised biography of the Spaniel that belonged to poet Elizabeth Barrett Browning, sold 19,000 copies in its first six months.

Yet Virginia disliked the work – she had written it for light relief after finishing *The Waves* and feared it made her look like a 'ladylike prattler'. However, critics have pointed out that it's not necessarily as frivolous as the subject matter might suggest. Some highlighted its apparent social commentary (while Flush is proud of his purebred lineage, the mongrels in the book seem happier and freer). Others have noted the parallels between Flush and Virginia's own golden Cocker Spaniel, Pinka, who modelled for the front cover. Pinka was a gift from Virginia's lover, Vita Sackville-West (see page 97); the dog was the offspring of Vita's pet, Pippin.

Pinka wasn't Virginia's first dog. This title went to scruffy grey Shag, who was sent by train to join her family at their Cornish summer home in

July 1892. Expecting an Irish Terrier, instead they received an odd-looking cross between a Collie and a Skye Terrier. In spite of this Shag was beloved by Virginia and her siblings, and in 1905 Virginia immortalised him in her second published essay, 'On a Faithful Friend': '[he was] a sociable dog, who had his near counterpart in the human world. I can see him smoking a cigar at the bow window of his club, his legs extended comfortably, whilst he discussed the latest news on the stock exchange with a companion.'

The family's next dog was Jerry, bought for Virginia and her siblings following their mother's devastating death. Then there was Hans, a Boxer rescued from Battersea Lost Dogs Home, whom Virginia taught to put out the matches she lit for her cigarettes (she would subsequently teach all her dogs the same trick).

In 1919, after Virginia and Leonard had moved to Monk's House, they acquired a mixed-breed Terrier named Grizzle. Their final dog together, succeeding Pinka, was a black-and-white Cocker Spaniel named Sally who dozed on the sofa each evening as they listened to their records. Sally outlived Virginia, but not Leonard. He owned at least one more dog, an obedient black-and-white Shetland Sheepdog named Merle.

The Politico's Pooches

LADY LONDON- DERRY AND HER DOGS

Mount Stewart, County Down

In Mount Stewart's breathtaking gardens lies the sarcophagus of the woman who created them: Edith, Marchioness of Londonderry (1878–1959). An influential socialite who campaigned for women's suffrage, Edith, Lady Londonderry led a fascinating life, and many of her stories are carved into the memorial. There's the insignia of the Women's Legion, which she created in 1915, and the shield of the Red Cross, perhaps referencing the Officers' Hospital she helped establish in her home. Other tableaus hint at her domestic life, and prowling through them are lots and lots of dogs.

For at Mount Stewart you might have found a Dachshund in the Little Dining Room, waiting for a treat, or had to shove a Scottish Deerhound from a sofa before taking your seat. Outside, Pekingese may have been spotted by the ponds, sitting upon the steps specially designed for smaller dogs to allow them easier access to the water. Edith, Lady Londonderry photographed her pets playing around the grounds, and either she or her daughter Mairi posed them for fun shots, tucking them in bed, the sheets pulled up to their chins. In the gardens, where the burial ground is as important to the design as the vibrant flowers, are tablets in memoriam to Edith, Lady Londonderry's beloved pets.

Left: *Edith, Lady Londonderry with her Favourite Hound, Fly* by Philip Alexius de László, 1913.

The Greats

BOB PARSONS, MICHAEL CLAYDON AND THEIR GREAT DANES

Newark Park,
Gloucestershire

Right: A portrait of Bob with Trudy in the grounds of Newark, commissioned by Michael for Bob's 70th birthday and painted by local artist Rob Collins.

A visit to Bob Parsons and Michael Claydon at Newark Park also a meant a visit to their Great Danes. You might have seen them bounding towards you along the driveway or stealing a plate of sausages at a dinner party.

When American architect Bob (1920–2000) heard about Newark Park, then in disrepair, he felt it would be the perfect restoration project. But Newark was far too big for one person, so Bob acquired a Great Dane named Trudy. She had a dedicated 'boudoir' on the second floor and wore Bob's cast-off jumpers to keep warm in winter. When Trudy passed away, Bob and Michael – who had since moved in – decided the house could not be without a Great Dane. They adopted many more and the animals quite literally made their mark on Newark. One, Misty, learnt to open the round, wooden door handles with her mouth (some of her her teeth marks are still visible). This led her to Max; the two were normally kept separate to avoid breeding, but soon after their meeting Portia came along…

Michael describes Max, a Harlequin, as 'absolutely amazing', but also nervous and mischievous. They once left him in the car while at dinner and returned to find the seat foam everywhere. 'Miraculously, the insurance company paid out for "accidental damage"'.

The last Great Dane of Newark was 'extraordinary' Boston, who lived to be 13 and survived Bob.

The Philanthropist's Family

LORD AND LADY NUFFIELD'S SCOTTIE DOGS

Nuffield Place, Oxfordshire

Left: A painting of four Scotties from Lord and Lady Nuffield's collection. Pen and ink drawing by Meta Plückebaum, 1950.

Scottie-loving Lord Nuffield, or William Morris, was a philanthropist and motor-car manufacturer. He began as a 15-year-old bicycle repairer and maker, working from a repair shop in his parents' home and went on to make his fortune in motor cars (though he never liked the most famous car associated with his firm, the Morris Minor). William was a talented cyclist, too, sometimes riding from Oxford to Birmingham and back in a day to pick up bike parts for special repair jobs. He was also a member of a cycling club and it was here that he met Elizabeth Anstey, whom he married in 1903. The couple didn't have children, and William left much of his fortune to charitable causes and Oxford institutions; despite their fortune they were a frugal couple who lived simply.

William and Elizabeth were also fond of their Scottie dogs, and they often owned a few at a time. Today Nuffield Place pays homage to the couple's love of these animals: in paintings and photographs; in models balancing on top of a wireless; and even in the carpets – Lady Nuffield's bedroom and downstairs the carpets bear distinctive stains caused by overexcited Scotties who couldn't make it to a more suitable toilet.

The Star Employee

KITE THE SHEEPDOG

Orford Ness,
Suffolk

Kite the Collie has a rather enviable start to his working day: a gentle boat ride across the River Ore to Orford Ness National Nature Reserve, where he and Shepherd Andrew Capell look after a flock of 140 sheep.

Kite started working for the National Trust in 2012, when he was one year old. Back then he could work with sheep, goats and geese but, as is typical, it took three more years of training before his sheepdog skills were completely up to scratch – 'a year for each leg', as Andrew puts it. Kite is now very privileged to be the only dog (aside from assistance dogs) allowed on the Ness, because of its many fragile habitats. In fact his work is vital in helping the Trust look after the flat, open marshes here; the grazing sheep keep the grass at the varied heights required by breeding and nesting birds, and it's Kite who makes sure that the sheep go to the right place at the right time.

After a long day at work, Kite enjoys going for a dip. Pools of water can pop up all across the Ness's marshes (another reason, aside from the well-grazed grasses, that birds like it here) but you're equally likely to find Kite splashing about in a water trough or 'most likely, a dirty ditch' says Andrew.

Kite loves his job and is possibly the hardest working staff member at Orford Ness – he even dreams about running the sheep. Says Andrew, 'He makes little sounds and his legs go crazy!'

Right: Kite
surveying his lands
at Orford Ness.

'OUTSIDE OF A DOG, A BOOK IS A MAN'S BEST FRIEND. INSIDE OF A DOG, IT'S TOO DARK TO READ.'

GROUCHO MARX

The Flying Farmers

DAN JONES, NEL, TIAN, MASK AND KIM

Parc Farm, Great Orme

Dan Jones and his working dogs have made the news twice: once when they moved into Parc Farm on the Great Orme in 2016 after the Trust launched a highly publicised search for a new farmer. The second time was when one of his dogs, a Collie called Tian, was knocked over Great Orme's coastal cliffs by a rambunctious sheep.

Dan watched as Tian disappeared over the side, knowing that rocks and sea lay 12m (40ft) below. Nervously, he peered down – only to spot an unharmed Tian swimming in the water. Dan phoned a rock climber friend, who used his equipment to rescue Tian. The miraculous survival story even made the national news.

Tian is one of four dogs who work on the 865-acre (350ha) Great Orme. His colleagues are fellow Collies Nel and Mask, and Kim, a New Zealand Huntaway. Their roles are vital for conservation. Great Orme's limestone cliffs are home to many rare species, including the Great Orme berry and Goldilocks aster. But the ground here is tricky to manage and before Dan arrived some areas had not been grazed for many years. Now Dan and his dogs ensure the farms' flocks of Lleyn and Herdwick sheep adhere to a strict grazing plan, the Collies keep watch to ensure the sheep stay in each area for the optimum amount of time to allow these important plants to flourish.

Right: Dan with Tian and Nel on the Great Orme.

The Unchained

DJANGO

Plymbridge
Woods and
Saltram, Devon

Handsomely rugged with his shaggy locks
and long, chocolate beard, Django the German
Wire-haired Pointer could be the poster pooch for
dogs of the great outdoors. It's perhaps no surprise,
then, that he's been a Ranger dog for the National
Trust since 2014, when he was just a puppy. Back
then, he and his human, fellow Ranger Douglas
Munford, were based at Buckland Abbey in Devon.
Nowadays they are usually found exploring the
ancient oak woodland at Plymbridge on the edge
of Plymouth, or patrolling Saltram's expansive
parkland (once a source of income for the
former inhabitants, Saltram remains a
working estate today).

Here Django is in his element. You'll generally
find him racing other dogs to the balls thrown for
them, running through his repertoire of tricks in
exchange for a meaty treat, or swimming at his very
favourite spot, an estuary beach on the River Plym.

His duties in the Ranger team are many and
varied, but he's particularly good at making sure
none of their equipment gets lost: 'If you put your
gloves down, he'll be sure to pick them up and run
around with them to let you know where they are,'
says Douglas. 'Occasionally he'll give them back.'

Left: Django during
a quieter moment
of repose.

The Hostess's Hounds

MRS GREVILLE AND HER DOGS

Polesden Lacey, Surrey

Right: A studio portrait of Mrs Greville and her white Collie, Tyne, in 1887.

In the grounds of Polesden Lacey, close to the peaceful Rose and Ladies' Gardens, is a dedicated pet cemetery. Here stand 17 memorials to the beloved dogs of Mrs Margaret Greville (1863–1942), an Edwardian society hostess who was close friends with three generations of the Royal Family, including King George VI and Queen Elizabeth, who honeymooned at Polesden Lacey in 1923.

Mrs Greville's dogs (mostly Pekingese and Terriers) have become intertwined with people's memories of Polesden Lacey. One local recalled how Mrs Greville liked to sit at a table at her front door with a particular dog upon her lap. School children – who visited for an annual summer party she hosted for local nearby schools – remember how Mrs Greville would sing and the dog would join in. Richard Dallimore, who came to Polesden as a young boy in the summer of 1936, remembers how Mrs Greville suggested he walk her dogs instead of staying for coffee with the adults, and how four or five accompanied him and the servants as they explored the grounds and, later, the mansion's opulent interiors. The latter was not an unusual occurrence – by all accounts, Mrs Greville's dogs would run riot within the mansion, seemingly more precious to her than even the prized collection of valuable Fabergé.

The animals often appeared in newspaper and magazine articles too. In November 1910, a profile in *The Hostess* mentions Mrs Greville's five Pekingese and 'handsome white Collie', and is illustrated with a picture of her on Polesden's steps with one of the Pekingese in her arms. It also pays particular mention to 'dainty' Cho (1908–24) 'who never leaves its mistress and has a decided personality – not to say temper – of its own' (Cho's gravestone is more euphemistic, describing their personality simply as 'lively'). Two years later, an article appeared in *Madame* discussing how Mrs Greville had arrived at her home in Charles Street, London, for one of the biggest events of the year, bringing with her a 'large family of pedigree Pekingese pets'. Over ten years later the fascination had not diminished; in 1925, *Sketch* discussed the changing habits of London's renowned dog walkers as they move from Hyde Park to Green Park, Mrs Greville and her white West Highland Terrier Rip among them.

There is also an 18th grave within Polesden Lacey's grounds: a simple slab commemorating Mrs Greville, forever close to her beloved pets.

Left: One of Mrs Greville's Pekingese dogs on a chair at Polesden Lacey.

The Ever-faithful Friend

DRUM AND PATRICK LICHFIELD

Shugborough, Staffordshire

'You rarely saw Lord Lichfield without his dog Drum,' said Corinne Caddy, former Product Development Officer at Shugborough. The sprawling Staffordshire estate was home to Patrick Lichfield, the renowned royal and society photographer, who had an apartment, including a studio, on the grounds. For the last seven years of his life, he was accompanied here by his faithful black Labrador.

Drum was not Patrick Lichfield's first canine companion. He owned many dogs and would frequently photograph himself with his pets; one self-portrait was included on a calendar he shot of celebrities and their dogs; another still hangs in the hallway of his apartment.

In his autobiography, Patrick declares that 'professional photographers reserve the right to tamper with the truth a little here and there, in pursuit of private visions. Reality's rather relative at the best of times; all we can offer is one aspect at a time, one angle, one story from amongst thousands.' And yet, the story his images tell when it comes to his dogs – one of devotion, of a special relationship between master and faithful hound – is very real. Drum was so devoted that when Patrick died from a stroke aged 66, the dog attended his master's funeral.

Left: Patrick Lichfield with one of his dogs in the grounds of Shugborough.

*Souvenirs
From Afar*

THE DOGS OF VITA SACKVILLE-WEST

Sissinghurst, Kent

Left: Vita
Sackville-West's
work *Faces* is a
celebration of
dog breeds and
describes Vita's
many encounters
with them.

In 1926, the writer and garden designer Vita Sackville-West (1892–1962) was introduced to 'the dullest dog I ever owned'. The unfortunate hound was a Saluki named Zurcha – 'yellow one' in Arabic – and had been gifted to her by the traveller and diplomat Gertrude Bell. Vita was staying with Gertrude in Baghdad on her way to meet her husband, Harold Nicolson, who was a diplomat in Tehran at the time. Inspired by Gertrude's own collection of 'desert dogs', Vita fancied a companion for her onward journey; sadly the 'completely spiritless' Zurcha proved useless in this regard, for she was 'faithful only to the best arm-chair'.

The story of Zurcha appears in one of Vita's last works, *Faces: Profiles of Dogs* (1961). The book is a celebration of dog breeds, of their temperaments and of Vita's encounters with them. She talks of Mr Egg the Schnauzer who 'spent most of his time lying in the middle of a village street, watching the traffic go by'; of 'hugely alarming' but kindly Great Danes; of how Afghan Hounds remind her of 'A sweet old lady, providing crumpets for tea. Aunt Lavinia, who nourishes a secret passion for the vicar.'

Faces also features the stories of the mongrels Vita had 'owned, or been owned by': there is the one who 'made her way into my house in Constantinople and … gave birth to a litter of puppies on the drawing-room sofa'; the 'dreadful little object' who followed her home from a bazaar in Tehran; and Micky, a Turkish dog who came back to England with her.

Vita and Harold's home at Sissinghurst still contains an homage to the dogs she owned and loved. In the woodland just south of the Lower Lake is a cemetery dedicated to three: Marthan (1937–48), Dan (1958–61) and Rollo (1948–60). The latter was an Alsatian, which seems to have been one of Vita's favourite breeds; in *Faces*, she described them as, 'beautiful, noble, intelligent and devoted'.

And then there were her Cocker Spaniels, a breed she believed to be loving and cheerful. There was Judy, a birthday gift from Harold in 1920, Sally, the dog her lover Virginia Woolf would ask her to bring on visits, and Pippin, who gave birth to a litter that included the dog who would become the Woolfs' beloved Pinka (see page 72). Pippin, a golden Cocker Spaniel, had a litter at the same time as Vita's Persian cat. Their offspring happened to be the same colour, and so, 'The Spaniel used to steal the kittens and deposit them amongst her own offspring, suckling them all indiscriminately, and I would swear that the little dog grinned up at me whenever I went to sort them out.'

Right: Vita and Alsatian in the study at Sissinghurst, photographed by John Gay (1948).

The Stick Seekers

BIGGLES AND BRAMBLE

Slindon Estate, West Sussex

Most of the time, National Trust dogs are important staff members, helping us look after our places. Then there are the times when, like Bramble of Slindon Estate, they get hungry and snack on the day's first sighting of a Brimstone butterfly – right in front of the Trust's butterfly guru, Matthew Oates. 'We think she thought it was a crisp,' sighs Katie Archer, Slindon's Lead Ranger and Bramble's so-called 'boss'.

Cheese-loving, lemon-and-white Bramble is one of two working Cocker Spaniels to help out in Slindon's 3,460 acres (1,400ha) of woodland, downland, farmland and parkland. Her partner in crime is black-and-white Biggles, who gained experience at nearby East Head and Woolbeding countryside before he and his owner, Area Ranger Lisa Trownson, moved to Slindon. Visitors might spot him riding around in the tractor, though if he had his way he'd be sitting on the accelerator ('After a quick discussion we came to the agreement that this isn't the best idea,' says Lisa). He's also good at making sure meetings keep to time – the Rangers know when it has overrun because they'll suddenly find him lap-hopping (generally in search of the person closest to the biscuit tin).

Left: Biggles on the run.

Both Spaniels also work closely with volunteers, who might be coppicing, fencing and much more. And both also love sticks. Biggles' favourite place at Slindon is the woods, as it's home to the greatest selection, and he'll often spend a day choosing the best one. Once he's chosen, 'ninja Spaniel mode gets switched on' as he chooses a very secret hiding spot for his selected stick, explains Lisa. 'If he catches you watching then he has to turn at least 90 degrees to choose a new direction or location.' Bramble, on the other hand, is less cagey with her sticks and uses them to involve new volunteers: 'When they feel at a loss for what to do next, she brings them a stick,' says Katie. We are unable to confirm whether these are the sticks Biggles has so carefully hidden.

Right: Bramble gallivanting through the water. He will play with a ball just as readily as a stick.

'A DOG WILL TEACH YOU UNCONDITIONAL LOVE. IF YOU CAN HAVE THAT IN YOUR LIFE, THINGS WON'T BE TOO BAD.'

ROBERT WAGNER

The Aspiring Thespian

ELLEN TERRY, HENRY IRVING AND FUSSIE

Smallhythe, Kent

In the 1880s, the renowned actress Ellen Terry received a rather unusual delivery at the Lyceum's stage door: two Fox Terriers. They were later christened Drummie and Fussie, and Fussie would go on to become something of a fixture at the London theatre.

Ellen fell for the breed after seeing a painting of one belonging to the jockey Fred Archer who found Ellen a Fox Terrier with 'a very good head, a first-rate tail, stuck in splendidly, but his legs are too long. He'd follow you to America.' Indeed Fussie would later join Ellen on the Lyceum Theatre company's tours of the United States.

This company, which Ellen was a part of from 1878–1902, was managed by fellow actor Henry Irving. The two were very close and Ellen gifted Fussie to Henry, who loved the dog, possibly more than any human. Fussie accompanied Henry to restaurants, theatre performances and on holiday, and he had his own chair in Henry's dressing room at the Lyceum. Ellen recalled how Henry won Fussie's affection with 'tomatoes, strawberries, [and] "ladies' fingers" soaked in champagne'.

At least twice during the company's tours of the States, Fussie made unplanned appearances on stage. Then in 1888, the theatre company headed out on another six-month tour, but Fussie was accidentally left behind at Southampton station. Unable to join the actors across the Atlantic, Ellen said that, 'He found his way back from there to his own theatre in the Strand, London.' On his return

Left: Ellen Terry with Fussie and Drummie, 1889.

to England, Henry celebrated being reunited with
the Terrier at a restaurant, where Fussie promptly
snaffled Henry's personal order of mutton.

Fussie lived for the stage and his stomach,
and these would be the cause of his death in
1897. They were at a Manchester theatre, when,
according to Ellen, a carpenter placed 'his coat
with a ham sandwich in the pocket, over an open
trap on the stage. Fussie, nosing and nudging
after the sandwich, fell through and was killed
instantly. When they brought up the dog after the
performance, every man took his hat off.' After the
show, Ellen found Henry back at the hotel, eating
dinner with Fussie curled up in his rug on the sofa
one last time; he was later buried in Hyde Park's
dog cemetery.

Fussie and Drummie were not Ellen's only dogs;
it's said she always liked to have the animals around
and they appear in many personal photographs
taken at Smallhythe, her country retreat. It is also
here that her daughter Edy's dog Ben is buried and
commemorated with a grave. Many a dog owner
will empathise with the conundrum they faced for
his epitaph, as he was so badly behaved they felt
they could not say 'good', and eventually settled
upon 'dear'.

*The Holiday
Hounds*

CHARLIE
AND BERRY

The South West
Countryside

When your day job involves long stints driving down the M5 motorway, or hiking a mile through snowdrifts to get to a holiday cottage, it's good to have a colleague or two to talk through your ideas and issues with. Good listeners perhaps; someone like Charlie and Berry the Labradors.

Yellow Lab Charlie has been coming to work with Jayne Smith, Holidays Manager in the South West, since 2012, when he was four years old. Five years later he was joined by black beauty Berry, then a puppy. A typical day might involve accompanying Jayne as she recces a walking route, testing out new biscuits for the cottages' welcome trays, or making a fuss over visitors. In 2017, Charlie also got the chance to star in a Facebook video promoting National Trust holiday cottages, and took the ensuing fame in his happy stride.

The Labs quickly got to know their patch. A number of the cottages are dog free and Jayne says that, 'They always know when we pull up at a cottage whether it is somewhere they can get out of the van or not.' That said, this hasn't stopped Charlie from pushing his luck when Jayne turns away; once they were staying overnight in a cottage with the leadership team and Jayne caught Charlie and the General Manager have a sneaky cuddle on the sofa – where dogs are most definitely not allowed. 'Both got told off!' she says.

Berry's friendly nature has also got her into a spot of bother. One day, as the trio were driving around, she noticed some of her human Ranger

Left: Charlie
relaxing in the
sun at Shedbush
Farmhouse holiday
cottage, Dorset.

Left: Berry
enjoying her first
proper snowfall.

friends and excitedly jumped out of the window
to greet them before the car had even stopped.

Jayne's job takes them to lots of Trust places in
the South West, but their very favourite is Exmoor;
the three love walking on the moor, swimming
in the river at Bossington and taking in the view
from the top of Dunkery Beacon. The parkland
at Newark Park, Gloucestershire (see page 78) is
another of their top spots and Charlie also loves
Burton Bradstock in Dorset – except when Jayne
joins him in the sea. 'Usually when I get in, he gets
out and barks at me!' she laughs.

When they're not keeping Jayne company
during her duties, Charlie – an old gentleman
these days – likes to snore away on an armchair,
his legs waving in the air. Berry, on the other hand,
is 'a hooligan – full of energy and doesn't stop.'
She might be found splashing about in water,
chasing Frisbees, carrying toilet rolls and books,
or pinching fruit from the kitchen.

The Playful Pup

THE HOARES AND THEIR DOGS

Stourhead, Wiltshire

In March 1910, Alda and Henry Hoare of Stourhead presented their son, Harry, with his 22nd birthday present: a black, wavy-coated Retriever, who had been bred in the family's kennels. Christened Sweep, he and Harry quickly became partners in crime: 'I can see Harry, in their joint youth, chasing him in every room we have,' reminisced Alda. Harry and Sweep remained devoted. On what would become Harry's final visit to Stourhead, while on leave from fighting in the First World War – a conflict that would cost him his life – Harry pecked his dear dog's head. 'I never saw him kiss an animal before,' Alda wrote.

Sweep captured many hearts besides Harry's. He slept in Alda's boudoir each night and the local village children loved him. Alda's cousin, Alda Sherwell, talked about the games they played: 'I taught him to go to the paper basket in the hall … The dog used to take out a bit of paper and then I'd chase him round and round until I caught him and he'd do that by the hour.'

Sweep was probably the last black dog Alda and Henry owned; Alda's failing eyesight meant that white dogs that were easier to see. One of these was an obedient Terrier named Nellie, nicknamed 'Queen'. This meant that at dinner, when it was time for dessert, Alda would ask their butler to 'put the Queen on the table.'

Right: Alda and Henry on their silver wedding day in October 1912, with Harry and Sweep.

*The Long
Legacy*

**PEEPS
AND JIM**

Tredegar House,
Newport

Tredegar House has been home to many animals, but undoubtedly the most unusual belonged to Evan Morgan (1893–1949). Eccentric to say the least, Evan dabbled in black magic and it's said the alcohol bill at his parties could reach £250 (the equivalent of around £15,000 today). His exotic menagerie included a boxing kangaroo, an alligator, a baboon and a parrot named Blue Boy, who is said to have once bitten the nose of Hermann Göring.

A predecessor of Evan's, Godfrey Charles Morgan (1831–1913), was more mainstream in both his lifestyle and his choice of pets, favouring dogs and horses. As a boy he would explore Tredegar's grounds with his Terrier, and he went on to become President of the Welsh Kennel Club, patronised and judged a number of dog shows in South Wales, and visited local sheepdog trials. His own pets – Barry, Friday and, his favourite, a Skye Terrier named Peeps – are buried in Tredegar's Cedar Garden.

Peeps – so-called because of the way he 'peeped' out from underneath his bushy grey eyebrows – is also commemorated alongside his master in a portrait by renowned portrait artist John Charlton; this can still be seen at Tredegar. This was one of five portraits Godfrey commissioned from

Left: Godfrey Morgan with Peeps, painted by John Charlton c.1896–7.

Charlton, another being a retrospective depiction of him at the Charge of the Light Brigade. Morgan was one of only two people from his division to return home unscathed; his horse, Sir Briggs, was also fortunate enough to escape harm and is buried alongside Peeps.

It seems likely, then, that Sir Godfrey would be pleased to know that dogs still call Tredegar home (or at least the office). Jim, a Border Collie, has been coming to work here as part of the Facilities team since 2007, when he was just six weeks old. He can often be seen riding around the estate in the off-road vehicles – 'there is nothing he likes to do more in the world,' says his owner, Facilities Manager Bob Sugden. In his downtime, Jim might be found at his favourite spot, the ornamental cascade on Tredegar's lake. 'He is fascinated by water and chases any that flows,' Bob reveals.

Jim's career at Tredegar has not been entirely without incident; he was once suspected of being a sandwich thief (though his involvement was never proven) and, on the hunt for a quiet spot to cock his leg, has also been known to mistake a man in green overalls for a tree.

The Enthusiastic Ambassador

TICTAC

Wicken Fen,
Cambridgeshire

Visitors to the Wicken Fen Nature Reserve Visitor Centre might notice a few strange-looking smudges around the bottom of the glass doors. These aren't left over by an inattentive cleaner, but instead are traces of one of the animals you might spot during a visit here: a German Shepherd named Tics, or Tictac when he misbehaves. Tics loves exploring Wicken Fen – so much that, in his hurry to get outside, he sometimes forgets the automatic doors won't be switched on out of hours, and has been sighted careening straight into the glass.

Originally a rescue dog, Tics has been coming to work at Wicken Fen with Ranger Carol Laidlaw since 2011. Carol looks after the hardy Konik ponies and Highland cattle that roam freely on the Fen, the first nature reserve the National Trust ever owned. The animals' grazing of the wetlands and grasslands is helping new plants become established here. Tics keeps Carol company when she's out and about, and can often be seen running alongside her and the Ranger team as they cycle around the Fen, or excitedly riding in one of the estate vehicles. Although not on the payroll himself, Tics has become something of an ambassador for the Trust: with his goofy smile and love of carrying a ball, visitors can't resist coming to say hello and find out more about what he and Carol are up to.

Right: Tics shaking himself off after a swim on the Fen.

The High-maintenance Hounds

THE SPANIELS OF WIMPOLE

Wimpole, Cambridgeshire

Rudyard Kipling's daughter, Elsie Bambridge (1896–1976) loved dogs from a young age (see page 18), and this continued into adulthood. When she and her husband, Captain George Bambridge, moved to Wimpole in 1937 they brought with them two Spaniels that they acquired while living in Europe when George was a diplomat. Issy heralded from Belgium, while her step-brother Primo was born in Madrid.

These were not the couple's first dogs together. In the early 1930s, they rented Attingham Park in Shropshire, which they shared with a Dachshund who enjoyed ridding the house of vermin. This habit concerned Elsie, who wrote to her father worrying that the little dog would make himself ill; Kipling allayed her fears by responding that Dachshunds' unusual body shape meant they could digest the mice easily, and weren't often sick.

Nor were Issy and Primo the first dogs to live at Wimpole. The Bambridge's predecessors, the Agar-Robartes, had King Charles Spaniels and Labradors, Leslie the Terrier and, in 1925, two dark Spaniels named Susie and Sally. At least one of their Spaniels had rather expensive taste. One photograph shows them sleeping on an armchair in Wimpole's Long Gallery. Part of a set of six, two of these armchairs came up for auction in 2011 with a reserve of £120,000–180,000. That's one impressive dog bed.

Left: A Spaniel snoozing at Wimpole.

BIBLIOGRAPHY

Curran, Jane, 'Car Manufacturer Wiliam Morris', BBC, 11 November 2009

Nixon, Caroline, 'Nuffield The Man' (Nuffield International Farming Scholars, May 2010).

'Cooking with dogs: How man's best friend powered the kitchens of the past', National Trust website. Accessed 27 May 2018.

Cummins, Bryan D. *Our Debt to the Dog: How the Domestic Dog Helped Shape Human Societies* (Carolina Academic Press, 2013).

Jesse, Edward, *Anecdotes of Dogs* (H.G. Bohn, 1858).

Tearle, Oliver 'A Short Analysis of Rudyard Kipling's "The Power of the Dog"', *Interesting Literature*, February 27 2018.

Lycett, Andrew, *Rudyard Kipling* (Hachette, 2015).

Ricketts, Harry, *The Unforgiving Minute: A Life of Rudyard Kipling* (Chatto & Windus, 1999).

Kennedy, Maev, 'Margaret Hardman: a forgotten Edwardian talent emerges', *Guardian*, Sunday 14 March 2010.

Hagerty, Peter, 'The Continuity of Landscape Representation: The Photography of Edward Chambré Hardman (1898–1988)', May 1999.

Dockter, Warren, 'Pigs, Poodles and African lions – meet Churchill the animal lover', *The Telegraph*, 27 January 2015.

Charlton, Corey, 'Bulldog spirit, but Churchill was a softie when it came to his Poodle', *Mail Online*, 18 November 2014.

Cryer, Max, *Every Dog Has Its Day* (Exisle Publishing, 2013).

YouTube, 'The Essence of Agatha Christie: Dogs'. Published 7 January 2014. Accessed April 3 2018. © Agatha Christie Limited 2014.

Hankins, Justine, 'Tail of two cities', *The Guardian*, 14 July 2001.

Poole, Roger, *The Unknown Virginia Woolf*, CUP Archive 1995.

Usui, Masami, 'Animal-Assisted Therapy in Virginia Woolf's *Flush: A Biography*'.

Berman, Jessica, *A Companion to Virginia Woolf* (John Wiley & Sons, 2016).

Woolf, Virginia, 'On A Faithful Friend'. Published in 'A Selection of Essays by Virginia Woolf'. Schoolwires.net. First published in the *Guardian*, 18 January 1905.

Caws, Mary Ann (ed), *Vita Sackville-West: Selected Writings* (St Martin's Press, 2015).

Sackville-West, Vita, *Faces: Profiles of Dogs*, (Harvill Press, 1961).

Potter, Beatrix, *The Journal of Beatrix Potter from 1881–1897*, (Penguin, 2012).

Linder, Leslie, *A History of the Writings of Beatrix Potter, Including Unpublished Work* (Penguin, 1971).

'Famous Fox Terriers No. 1; Thomas Hardy's Dog' on 'Forever Foxed', 21 November 2008.

Brottman, Mikita, 'Top dogs: 10 literary canines', *The Guardian*, 13 September 2014.

Brottman, Mikita, *An A-Z of Exceptional Dogs*, (William Collins, 2014).

Ray, Martin, *Thomas Hardy Remembered*, (Routledge, 2017)

Gray, Beryl, '"Nero c'est moi": Jane Welsh Carlyle and Her Little Dog' in *Carlyle Studies Annual*, Number 22, Spring 2006, pp. 181–211.

'Farewell, old pal', *Daily Mail*, 22 November 2005.

'Shugborough Hall to reveal the life of an earl', *Express & Star*, January 24 2011

Lichfield, Patrick, *Not The Whole Truth: An Autobiography* (Headline Book Publishing Plc, 1987).

Halifax, Justine, '"Ordinary" life as lord of the manor', *Birmingham Post*, 3 September 2010.

PICTURE CREDITS

INDEX

ABOUT THE AUTHOR

Amy Feldman is an editor for the National Trust. She is the author of *Cats of the National Trust* as well as a number of National Trust guidebooks.

ACKNOWLEDGEMENTS

This book would not have been possible without the incredible National Trust staff and volunteers who took the time to talk to me about their dogs, helped me find information about their places' history, humoured me with my requests for photographs and much more. A huge thank you to Michael Claydon for taking the time out of your day to regale me with tales of Newark Park and the wonderful Great Danes, it was truly a pleasure. Thank you also to Joe at the Christie Archives and Mathew Prichard, Susie Thomson, the team at Dorset County Museum and Rob Collins. I am also hugely grateful to the team at the National Trust and Pavilion for all your support and indulging me as I spent months telling you dog stories, in particular Katie Bond, Claire Masset, Kristy Richardson and Peter Taylor.

As ever, thank you to John – this book wouldn't have happened without your support (and I know this is the first page you're reading). And finally to my parents and grandparents, because they didn't get a mention in my last book and were still its biggest advocates. Thank you for everything, always.

Left: Edgar 'Ted' Lister, who restored Westwood Manor in Wiltshire, and one of his beloved Old English Sheepdogs – all of whom he named Gelert.